TABLE OF CONTENTS

How To Promote Your Book Online & Offline Volume #2
Additional Promotional Strategies I Have Never
Revealed That Will Push Your Books To #1 Rankings!
©Copyright 2013 by Dr. Leland Benton

DISCLAIMER AND TERMS OF USE AGREEMENT:

(Please Read This Before Using This Book)

This information is for educational and informational
purposes only. The content is not intended to be a
substitute for any professional advice, diagnosis, or
treatment.

The author and publisher of this book and the
accompanying materials have used their best efforts in
preparing this book.

The author and publisher make no representation or
warranties with respect to the accuracy, applicability,
fitness, or completeness of the contents of this book. The
information contained in this book is strictly for
educational purposes. Therefore, if you wish to apply

Introduction – DIVERSIFY!!!

In preparing this book, I asked myself why so many authors do not know about the amazing strategy topics I will discuss today or the confusion that surrounds them. After all, none of them are NEW programs and most have been around for a long time in the publishing field. What is new is HOW I do them and HOW I have tweaked them to work better, which I am going to teach you.

The online forums help out but cannot provide enough information in a manner when it is needed. Like it or not, we are "stuck" with webinars or the dreaded "informational products" from the so-called gurus, who frankly in my opinion, are getting worse and worse as they struggle to find topics to present and over-charge their customers. Can you tell I am not a fan of informational products?

But think about it, that is exactly what every author does – sells information so now maybe we need to change our attitudes. NOT! It's a living!

The programs described herein are truly mindboggling and if you implement them correctly, you will literally see an explosion of book sales.

In volume #1, I gave various programs that would also increase your book sales exponentially but in this volume #2, ah…these are the strategies that I use to push my over 200-books published on Amazon alone to a five figure monthly income. Here is a list of what was presented in volume #1:

How To Promote Your Book Online & Offline Volume #1

Marketing & Promotions Checklist
EPUB Publishing Formats
Quantcast
Backlinks
Promo Book Trailers
Author Central
Book Tours
Audiobooks
Translations
Proof-reading & Editing
Email
Mobile Marketing
Automated Postcards
Pay Per View
Social Media Marketing
The Most Important Publishing Platforms

As you can see, it contained a good amount of information. So, where do we begin in Volume #2? It all begins in the mind…

Mindset

I am a behavioral scientist and mindset is an important human trait that defines our successes or failure. I practice a philosophy of "Give to Get" and choose to offer my time, talent and treasury to people that deserve to win. This is why I assist authors of all types.

With that said, I can do nothing for any author unless they have the proper mindset to succeed. The forums, where most of you come from, only work if everyone is pulling on the same oar and unfortunately not everyone is pulling on the same oar.

You have a very unique opportunity here to DIVERSIFY and offer a wide range of books in various genres. I will show you how. Click on the URL below and read some of the statistics affecting our industry.

http://selfpublishingresources.com/resources/books-news-and-publishing-industry-statistics/

NEVER rely on any one publishing platform EVER!

Now I know I sound like a broken record but if I succeed in teaching you anything then I hope it is to **DIVERSIFY** your publishing activities to the following five platforms and by doing so, these platforms also publish your books to the other important platforms listed under each platform:

Createspace - Standard: Amazon.com, Amazon Europe, Createspace Store. Expanded: Bookstores and Online Retailers, Libraries and Academic Institutions, Createspace Direct independent bookstores and book resellers.

https://www.createspace.com/

Smashwords - Apple iBookstore, Barnes & Noble, Sony, Kobo, Diesel, Baker & Taylor.

http://www.smashwords.com/

Lulu.com - Amazon .com US, UK, France, Germany, Italy, and Spain stores, $75 Ingram Catalog retailers Amazon.com, BN.com, local bookstores, etc, iBookstore.

http://www.lulu.com

BookBaby - iBookstore, Amazon Kindle, Barnes and Noble PubIt, Sony eReader Store, Kobo, Copia, Gardner Books, Baker & Taylor Bookstore, eBook Pie, eSentral.

http://www.bookbaby.com/

BookLocker - Amazon.com, BarnesandNoble.com PubIt, BooksaMillion.com and many other smaller, online bookstores, both domestic and foreign. Any bookstore with an Ingram account can pick up Ingram's feed.

http://publishing.booklocker.com/

This book is part of my ePublishing series designed to assist authors in reaching their publishing goals. They offer topic-specific instruction for all types of authors:

How to Promote Your Book Online & Offline Volume #1
How to Write a Kindle Book in Hours
How to Write Compelling Content
International Standard Book Numbers
Promoting Your Video Book Trailers
Publish with a Purpose
The ePubWealth Program
The ePubWealth Program ADVANCED

You can find these books by going online to the ePubWealth.com Library Catalog:
EPW Library Catalog Online
http://www.epubwealth.com/wp-content/uploads/2013/07/Leland-benton-private-turbo.pdf

EPW Library Catalog Download
http://www.filefactory.com/f/562ef3ea1a054f0a

The ePubWealth ADVANCED Program is an online course that is a continuing work in progress where it literally never ends. I offer hands-on instruction to authors of all types and experience using all the resources I have available here at ePubWealth plus my 31-years experience as a full service publisher and author. If you are interested in joining the class go here for more information:

http://www.epubwealth.com/epubwealth-advanced-program/

The class costs just $27/month and is very intense. If you wish to sign up go here:

https://www.paypal.com/cgi-bin/webscr?cmd=_s-xclick&hosted_button_id=RH9F934L5L2R4

Okay, so let's get at it…

Chapter 1 – Tried & True Book Content Strategies #1
The Amazon Hookup Program

What is Amazon Hook-Up?

It is a PPC spy program that takes advantage of Amazon's awesome $9-million monthly PPC buys on Google AdWords. By using the techniques that I teach you, you can "hook-up" your books to their targeted keywords and get free promotion for each and every one of your books. This is NOT a new program and PPC spying has been around since Google launched AdWords in 2001. Here is one of the biggest AdWords spy programs (note: do not buy this program...read on).

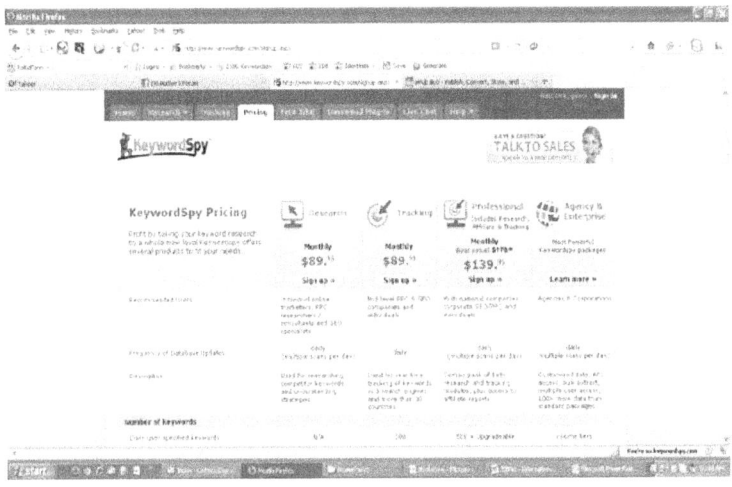

All of the top publishing house use The Amazon Hook-Up Program daily and so should you.

But I am going to show you a very low-cost way of doing the Amazon Hookup Program and then show you how to hookup your books to it.

You will need the following program:
SEMRush http://www.semrush.com/

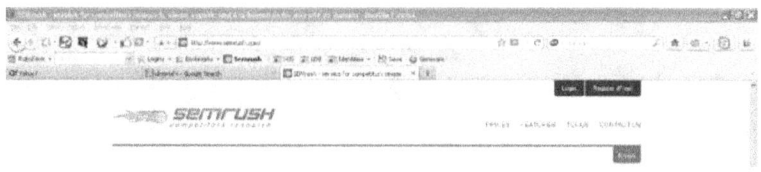

PROFESSIONAL SOFTWARE
FOR SEARCH AND MARKETING PROFESSIONALS

It costs $69.95/month; however, you can try it for just $79.95 for 1-month only and see if the Amazon Hookup Program is for you before you make a monthly commitment.

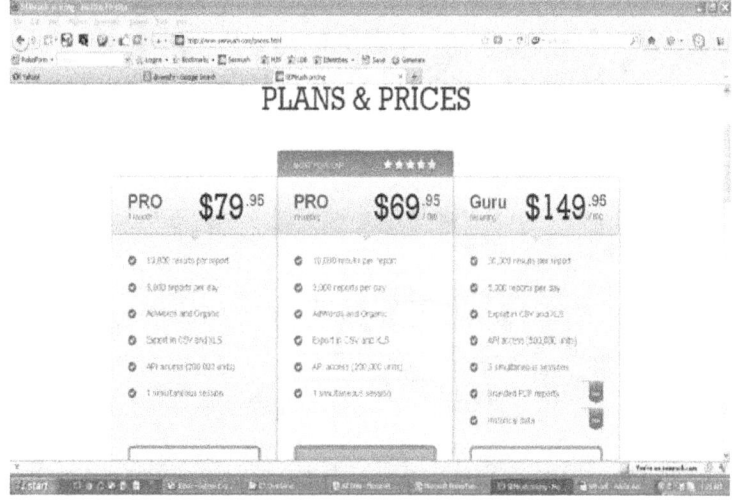

Now look at the screenshot below. In the lower left hand corner, notice the open ad box for Lululemon Fashions. I am going to use this as an example.

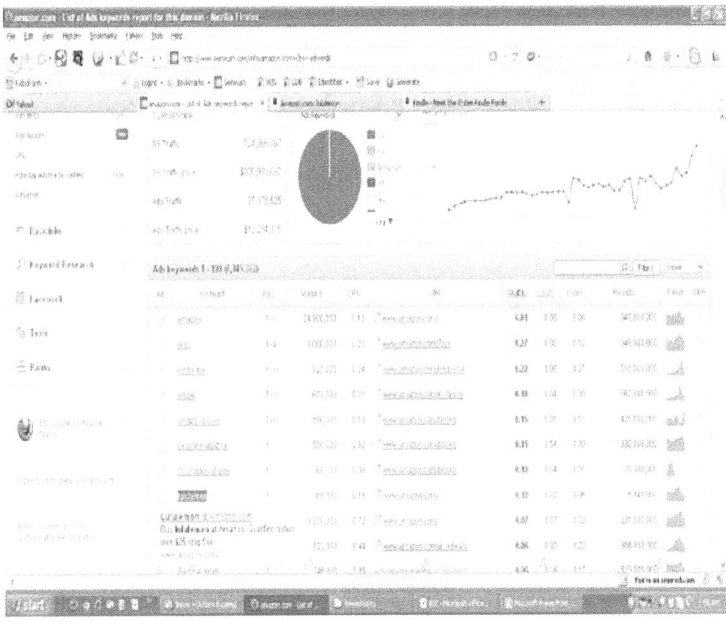

When you click on the Amazon AdWords ad for Lululemon you are taken to the screenshot below on Amazon.com. You always want keywords that take you to Amazon.com (not the Kindle Store) because the Amazon Hookup Program works best when the ads click through to Amazon.com and "all category" on the Amazon search engine.

In the screenshot below notice the book title "My Night with George Clooney" by Chelsea Henderson. Notice

13

that 823,000 people clicked on this ad and saw her book listing (see above screenshot next to Lululemon ad box).

A whopping 823,000 people saw that book listing and it is a Kindle book too (notice Kindle Edition next to the $2.99 price). The author made a mistake pricing the book at $2.99 but that is her problem. And she only has 5-reviews and 2-Likes. She is falling down on the job, people. She is ranked 518,000, which sucks for the amount of FREE exposure she is getting from Amazon Hookup. She should be below 10,000 in the rankings.

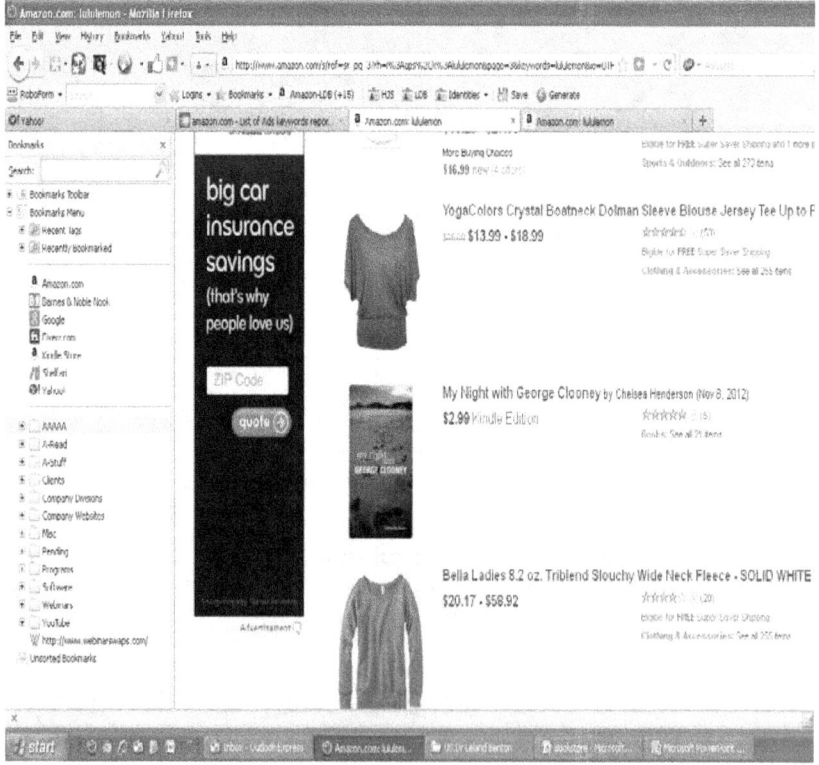

14

This is how you would hookup your book to this ad: when you publish your book in KDP make sure the keyword "lululemon" is one of the 7-keywords that Kindle allows!!!

lululemon
fashions
fashion trends
high fashion
simply fashion
fashion styles
fashion shopping

Steps to Doing "Keyword" Amazon Hook-Up

1. Sign up for a SEMRush.com account.
2. Login and click on the tab "Advertising Research" in the left hand column and then type Amazon.com in the search box.
3. Search for keywords that match your book and that are in the "ALL" category of the Amazon.com search engine. DO NOT USE THE KINDLE STORE SEARCH ENGINE!!!
4. Furthermore, make sure that the keyword selected does not have a huge amount of search results like the word "kindle".
5. Make sure your book's keyword that you have selected is listed as one of the 7-keywords allowed on the KDP Publishing platform.

Okay, now let's do another example using the keyword "kindle" just for demonstration purposes. Please do not use this example; it is just for demo purposes. Go to

Amazon.com and enter the word "kindle' in the search box.

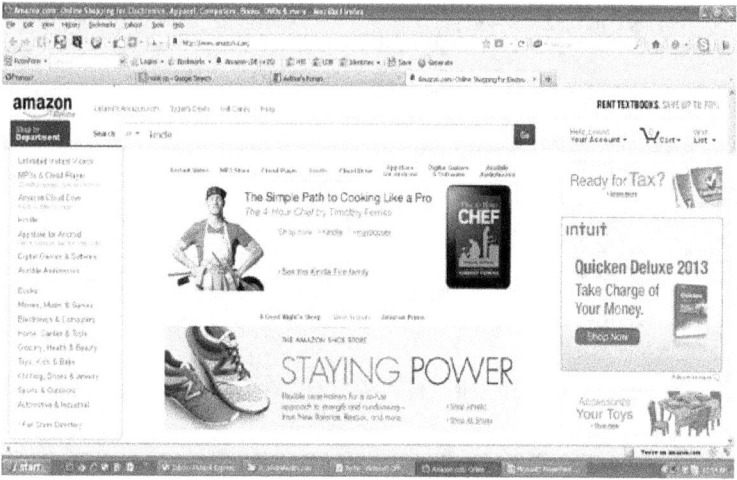

Here is what you get and when you scroll down the page you come to the first book listing, "The Complete Sherlock Holmes".

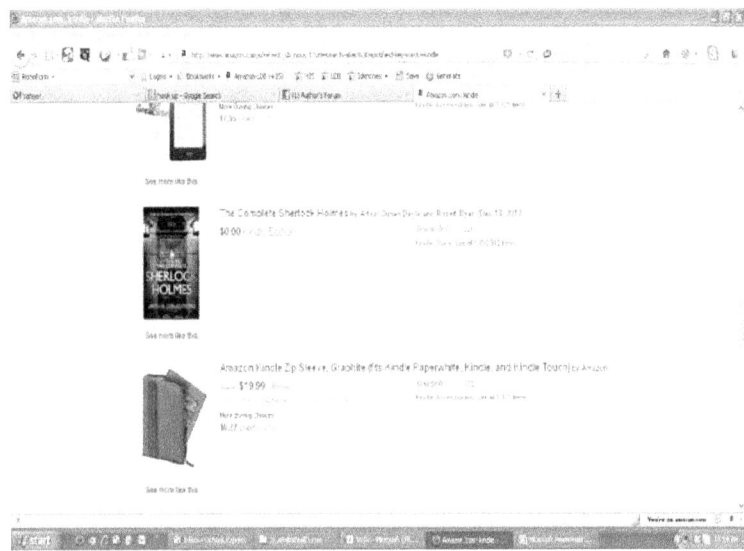

The second book listing is "Waking Up Married".

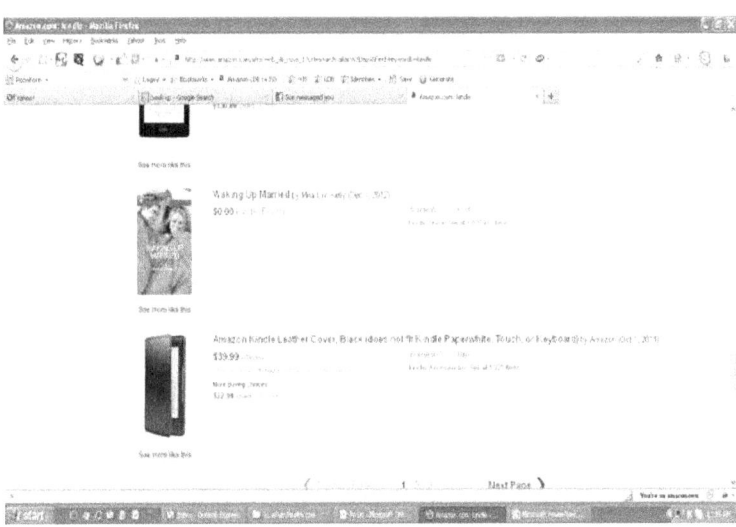

If we click through to the Kindle URL sales page we see that this book is a winner. It has 1165 reviews and 440 Likes...WOW!

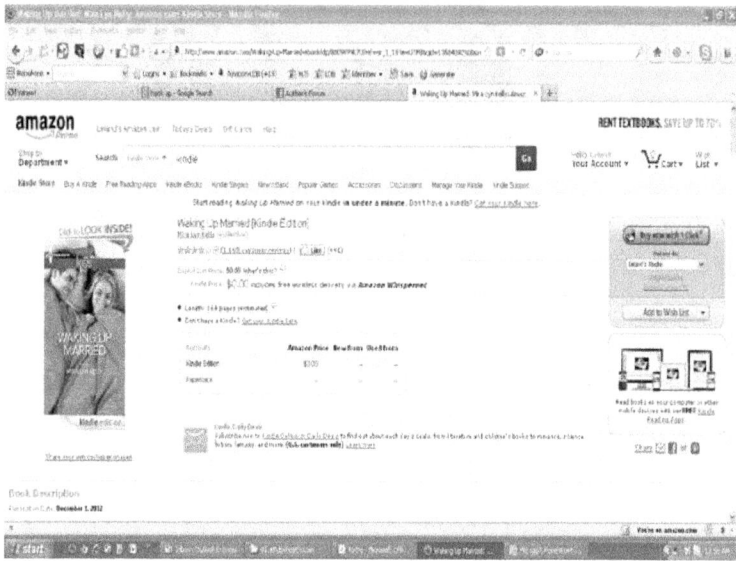

It is ranked #25 in the Kindle Store (enlarge the screen for better viewing.)

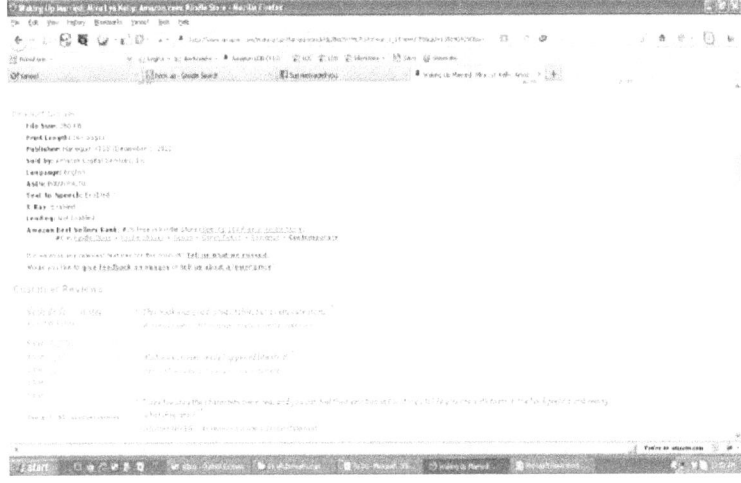

Now let's look at the Sherlock Homes book:

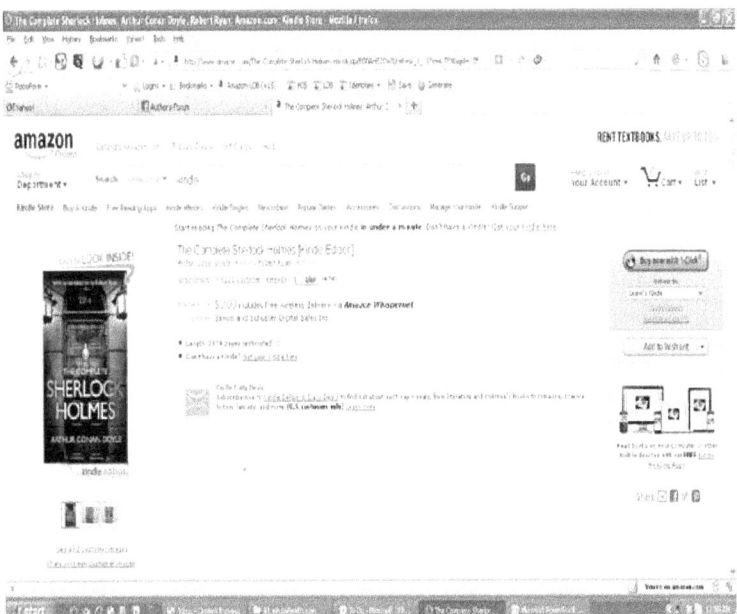

It has 221 customer reviews and 474 Likes and is ranked #17 in the Kindle Store. But why does this book have a better ranking than Waking Up Married? Let's go to Site Explorer http://www.opensiteexplorer.org/ and check.

Whoever did this is sheer genius. What this person did was "hookup" their book to the keyword "The Hunger Games," which is the number one rated book on Amazon.com and because of this they outranked the Waking Up Married book, which had way more reviews and Likes.

Okay the reason why you don't want to place the keyword "kindle" as one of your 7-keyowrds on the KDP platform is because it is too competitive showing almost 4 million results on the search engine ranking (see highlight below in the upper left hand corner.).

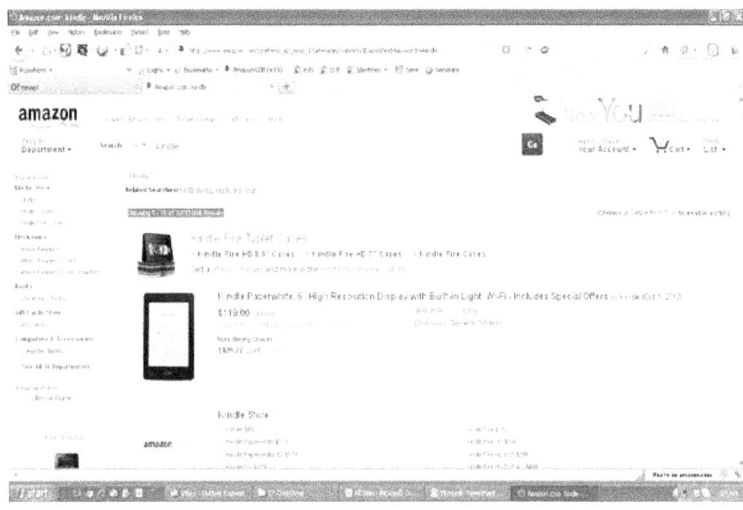

Try the Amazon Hookup program and see your book sales explode literally overnight.

Chapter 2 - Tried & True Book Content Strategies #2 OverDrive

OverDrive is a leading full-service digital distributor of eBooks, audiobooks, and other digital content. They deliver secure management, DRM protection, and download fulfillment services for publishers, libraries, schools, and retailers--serving millions of end users globally.

There are 138,000 lending libraries in the USA alone with average reader membership of 150-250 readers per library. This totals a marketplace of 34.5 million readers.

OverDrive | OneClickdigital | Freegal

What would you like to download today?

What device do you have? Click on your device for instructions

Enjoy thousands of free eBooks from the County of Los Angeles Public Library. Check out up to 10 titles at a time. Titles automatically expire - no late fees! You'll need:

- A County Library card in good standing
- A device or computer to read the eBooks (more on this below)
- Access to the Internet - you can even use the County Library Wi-Fi (in some cases)

You can apply for a publisher account at http://www.overdrive.com but fair warning; it isn't easy getting a Publishers account. If you are declined, don't worry; just use what is called book aggregators. Here are the best top three book aggregators:

http://www.ipgbook.com/
http://www.constellationdigital.com/
http://www.nbnbooks.com/

Directory of Lending Libraries Worldwide

Under the download portal here: http://www.filefactory.com/f/0b2c1210237b1afc, I have prepared a list of lending libraries worldwide along with a bunch of other goodies from my webinar on this same subject.

I am going to show you how to turn this resource into pure gold using a tried and proven method that you are familiar with – EMAIL MARKETING!

This program rocks and is passive, which means once you set it up; it runs on its own without you having to do anything else. But first, let's show you how Overdrive works using the greater Phoenix Digital Library as an example.

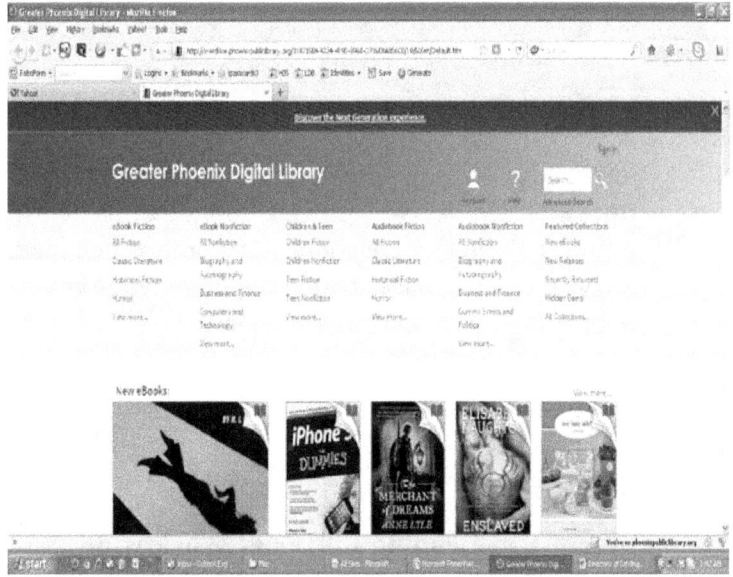

Look at the screenshot above and under eBook Fiction, we will click on "Humor," which takes us to this screenshot below:

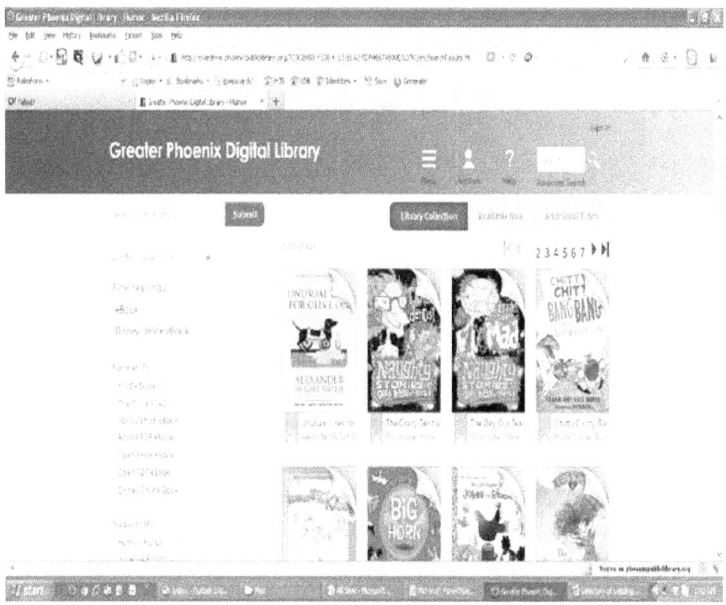

We will click on the first book "Unusual Use For Olive Oil" and we get the screenshot below. Notice in the right hand corner that there are only 3-copies to lend and none are available so if this is the book you wanted you would have to place a "hold" on it.

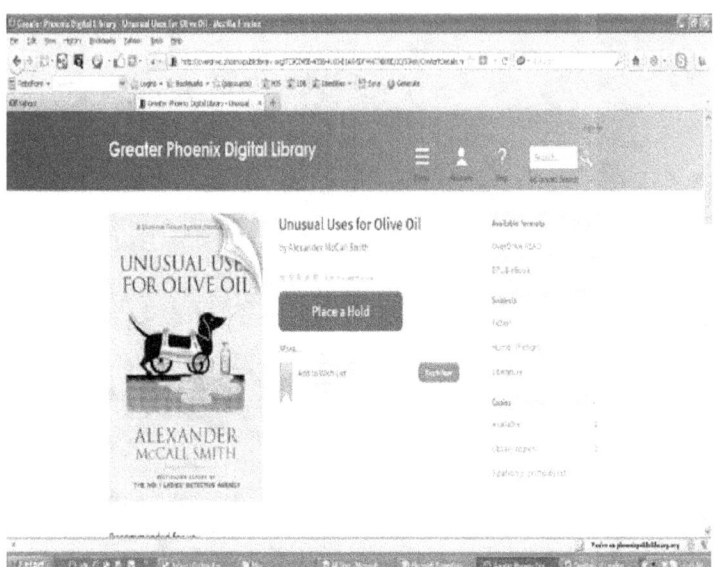

But, the alternative is the little green button in the middle of the screen which says "Buy It Now". If you click on this button a screen popup appears:

This is where you benefit because the customer goes to your sales page and buys your book rather than wait for it to become available for lending. Neat, eh?

Okay, now I am going to show you how to use my Directory of Lending Libraries Worldwide to make a fortune using email marketing.

Assumptions: You now have an Overdrive Publisher's account or book aggregator account and you now have a Directory of Lending Libraries Worldwide.

Needed: An Email sending platform and a list of email addresses. Go here:

Hypermail
http://tinyurl.com/hypermailplatform

List of Email Addresses go here;

EmailNations.com
http://www.emailnations.com

Send a text email or an HTML email announcing the lending libraries in their area first. Give them information first.

If you are mailing to a Los Angeles list, give them the lending libraries in the Los Angeles area.

Then ask them to look for your FREE book.

The email can look like this…

Hi [Firstname],

I want to make you aware of a FREE service available in your area. Here is a list of local Lending Libraries where you can go online and borrow ebooks for FREE!
Los Angeles County Public Library -- http://e-media.lapl.org/

Los Angeles Public Library (City) -- http://scdl.lib.overdrive.com/9B80D0C5-D85A-4F32-9AC8-D19C877FF4DF/10/363/en/Default.htm

I publish a list of lending libraries worldwide so click here to download the list for free:

http://tinyurl.com/endinglibrariesworldwide

And while you are at it, please feel free to check out my FREE ebook, "Howdie Doodie," which is a humor book about the fairy tales we tell our children that scares them to death.

Thanks,

Leland Benton, Author

Okay, when a customer clicks on this link: http://tinyurl.com/endinglibrariesworldwide, they are taken to a sign up box and captured into my autoresponder service:

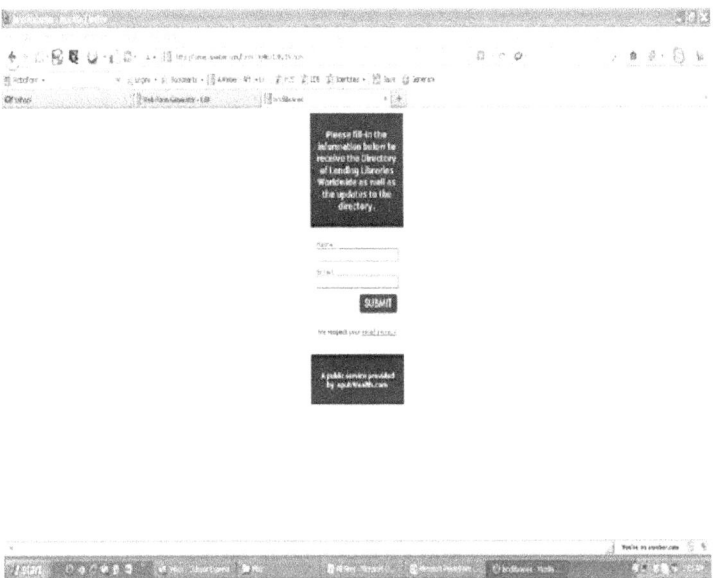

Once they fill-in the information and confirm their email address they are taken to the download portal. You now have compiled a list of customers to sell your books to.

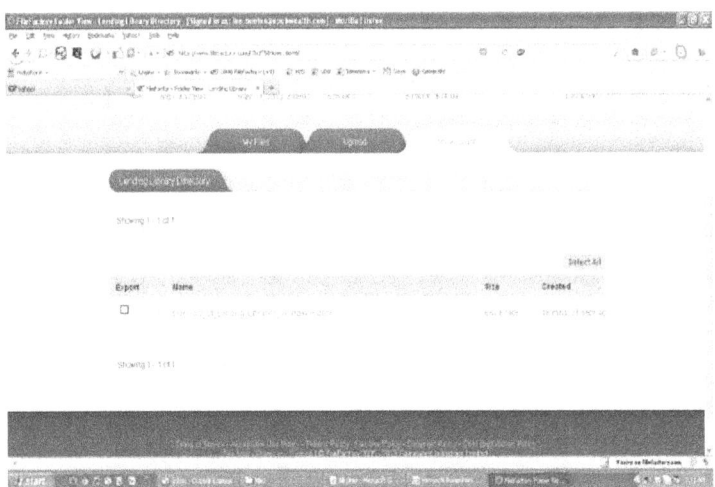

29

Chapter 3 - Tried & True Book Content Strategies #3 Backlinking

The Key of Getting Good Page Rank is Backlinks

Backlinks – the most important aspect of promotion using Link Profile Services, One Hour Backlinks and Ping Farm

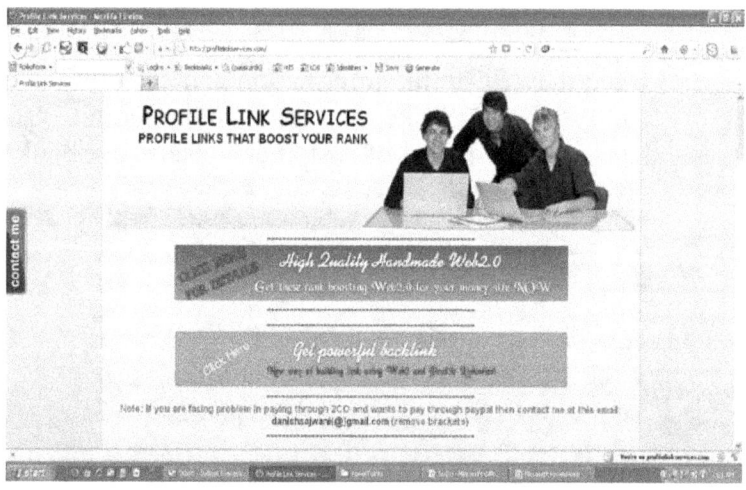

Profile Link Services is one of the best kept secrets of the web. They do a very remarkable job for a low price. There are two options available for 100 backlinks – link wheel @$30 and regular service @ $20.

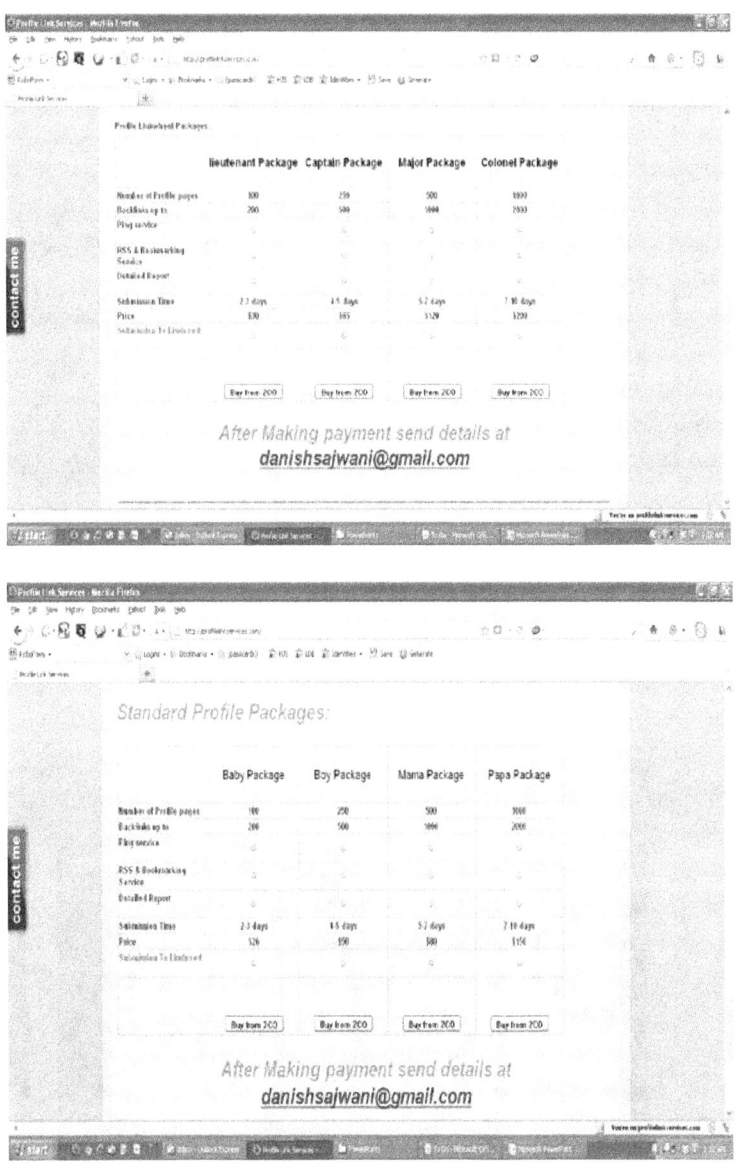

Profile Linkwheel Packages

	lieutenant Package	Captain Package	Major Package	Colonel Package
Number of Profile pages	100	250	500	1000
Backlinks up to	200	500	1000	2000
Ping service	✓	✓	✓	✓
RSS & Bookmarking Service	✓	✓	✓	✓
Detailed Report		✓	✓	✓
Submission Time	2-3 days	4-5 days	5-7 days	7-10 days
Price	$30	$65	$120	$200
Submission To Links red	✓	✓	✓	✓
	Buy from 2CO	Buy from 2CO	Buy from 2CO	Buy from 2CO

After Making payment send details at
danishsajwani@gmail.com

Standard Profile Packages:

	Baby Package	Boy Package	Mama Package	Papa Package
Number of Profile pages	100	250	500	1000
Backlinks up to	200	500	1000	2000
Ping service	✓	✓	✓	✓
RSS & Bookmarking Service	✓	✓	✓	✓
Detailed Report		✓	✓	✓
Submission Time	2-3 days	4-5 days	5-7 days	7-10 days
Price	$26	$50	$80	$150
Submission To Links red	✓	✓	✓	✓
	Buy from 2CO	Buy from 2CO	Buy from 2CO	Buy from 2CO

After Making payment send details at
danishsajwani@gmail.com

The following report is what you receive back in a couple of days:

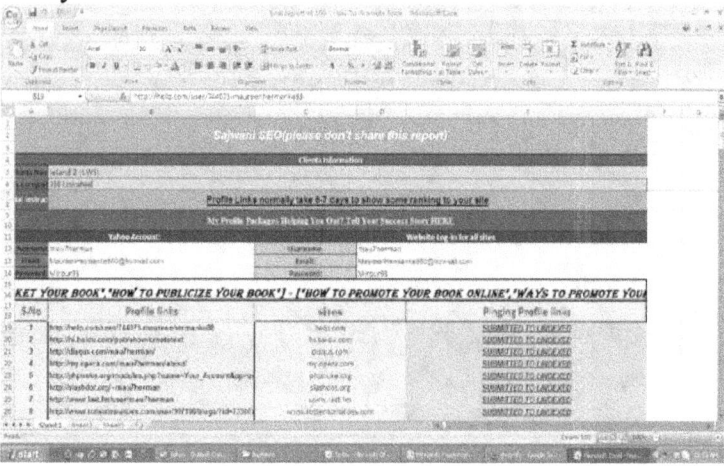

You then highlight the entire column called Profile Links and copy it. Then go to OneHourBacklinks.com and paste the copied column into the URL box (see screenshot below).

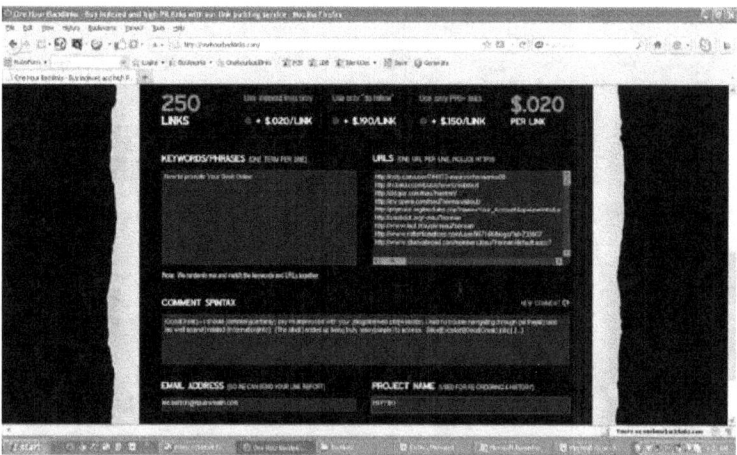

Under "Keywords" type in your keyword phrase then enter your email access and project name. In about an hour you will receive a report like the one below:

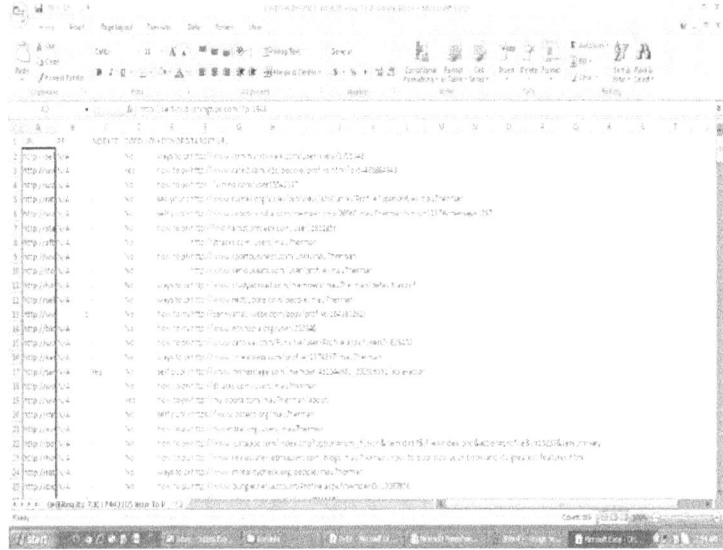

Highlight and copy Column A and then go to http://pingfarm.com and paste the entire Column A into the box as shown below at PingFarm.com.

Enter your keyword phrase and your RSS Feed (get one for free at Feedburner.com if you don't have one) and then click on the "Mass Ping" button.

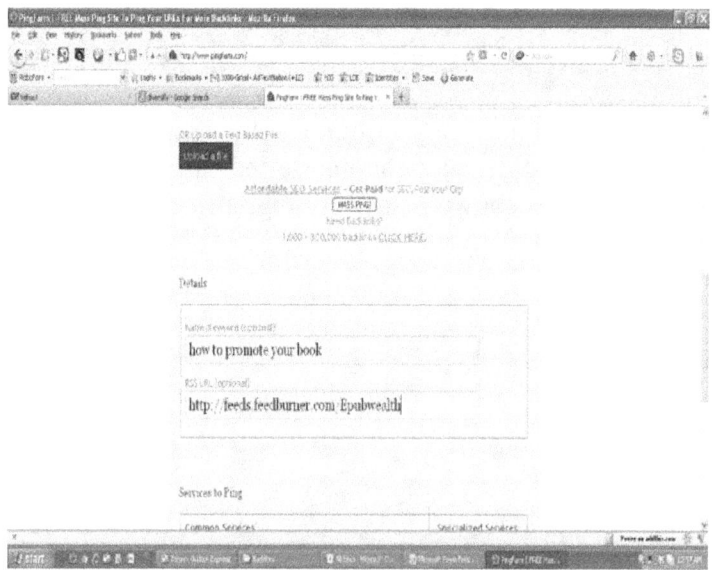

That is it in building over 100 backlinks to your book. You need to do this once a month in order to have consistency with the search engines.

Chapter 4 - Tried & True Book Content Strategies #4 Book Breaking

Bookbreaking- is a very simple but very effective concept. You take existing books and combine the content into a new book in part or in total.

I have published two books using the Bookbreaking technique, and then using the checklist I provided in the download portal listed in Chapter 2, I do a full blown promo campaign.

Book breaking works best on books that have a vast amount of content. Most Kindle books average 20-40-pages. I have Kindle books well over 200-pages and these are the ones I use to break into small books.

Kindle loves book breaking and doesn't even require that you unpublish the original, book.

The following books are books that I have used this technique on:

21st Century
Marketing Genius

It's All About the Amount of Ad Impressions You Place in the Marketplace!!

Dr. Leland Benton

Effective Email Advertising

Email Marketing is still the most cost effective form of online marketing!

A WEAPON
OF MASSIVE
CONSUMPTION

'CONSUMING ENTITIES ALWAYS LOSE'

DR. LELAND BENTON

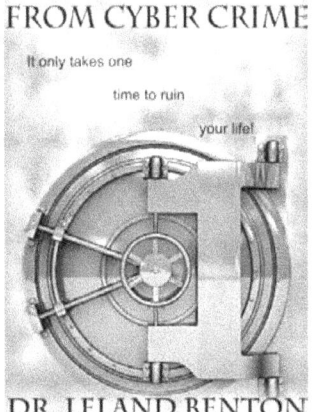

The books listed above should give you some good ideas about book breaking some of your existing books.

You can find these books by going online to the ePubWealth.com Library Catalog:
EPW Library Catalog Online
http://www.epubwealth.com/wp-content/uploads/2013/07/Leland-benton-private-turbo.pdf

EPW Library Catalog Download
http://www.filefactory.com/f/562ef3ea1a054f0a

Chapter 5 - Tried & True Book Content Strategies #5 Quotebacks

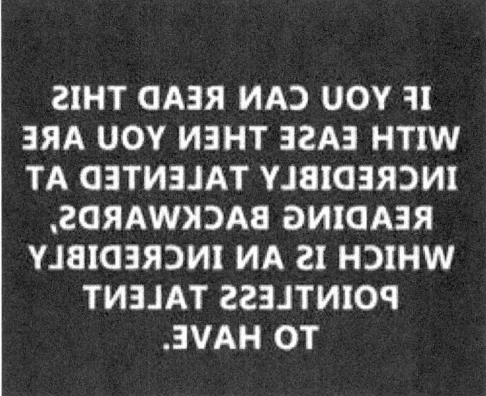

Quotebacks – You use existing articles from other others as content for your book where you give the author credit plus the URL to the article.

Be sure to quote the article in its entirety, i.e. I wrote most of the book "How to Choose a Good Trading System" using other author's articles including my own.

In fact, about 80% of the book is made up of quotebacks from other author's.

Under the fourth amendment, specifically "Republishing Rights", which Google uses all the time to keep things permanent on the Internet, this is completely legal.

Below is a screenshot that demonstrate what I am speaking about using "How to Choose a Good trading System". Notice that I used the articles exact URL:

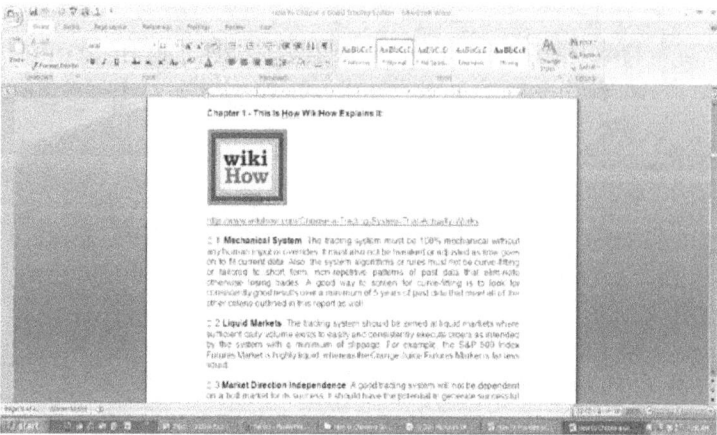

You must use the exact article in its entirety without any edits. It must include the author's bio if it is a part of the article and the article URL too. You can remove any graphics but disclosed that the graphics has been removed.

42

If you follow the instructions above then you do not need the author's permission nor are you in violation of any copyright laws. You are simply republishing the article.

Chapter 6 – Tried & True Book Content Strategies #6
Viral Images

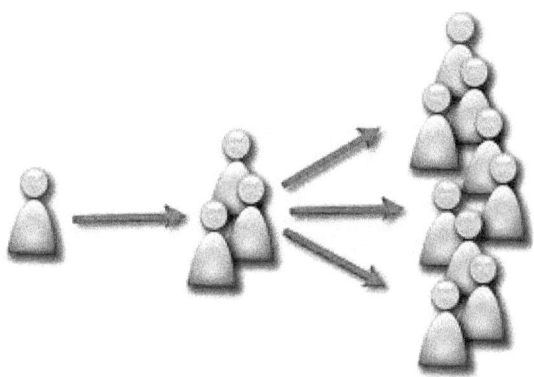

Viral Images rock! But they must be done correctly; otherwise it swiftly becomes an exercise in futility.

With viral images you can tap into social sites that send more referral traffic than Google, Linked In and YouTube combined.

Social sites give high authority backlinks, which benefit your Google rankings too.

Animated GIFs and memes get shared around the web and go viral just because of their creative and amusing nature.

In my book "Distraction Marketing" I demonstrate how funny emails go viral instantly and how to capitalize on that craze.

Viral images do the same thing; they go viral instantly if done correctly.

Where do you get the images? Here is a list of royalty free image sites:

Image Marketing Sites (Free Rights)
http://www.freephotosbank.com/
http://www.freejpg.com.ar/
http://visipix.dynalias.com/index_hidden.htm
http://www.burningwell.org/gallery2/main.php
http://tofz.org/
http://stock.diwiesign.com/
http://amygdela.com/stock/
http://www.zurb.net/zurbphotos/
http://energy.star29.net/store/
http://www.photogen.com/
http://www.freedigitalphotos.net/
http://www.sxc.hu
http://www.dreamstime.com/free-photos
http://office.microsoft.com/en-us/images
http://freerangestock.com

Here are some more royalty free sites…

- **Okaboo.com** - Free public domain and creative common pictures of everything on Earth. Free stock photos of places, people, animals and much more. Okaboo also makes it easy for you to add image credits back to the source. http://ookaboo.com/o/pictures/

Library of Congress -Digital image collection from the Library of Congress. Lots of public domain images. http://www.loc.gov/index.html

Foter.com - A great source of free quality images on everything. Easy to use and they provide a great way to easily add image and credits on your websites and blogs. http://foter.com/

AllPosters.com - AllPosters has millions of fantastic art and poster prints that you can use on your websites. http://www.allposters.com

FreeDigitalPhotos.net - A huge range of royalty free and premium stock photos and images to use anywhere. You need to publish a credit for the free images you use. http://www.freedigitalphotos.net/

Flickr - Flickr is a wonderful source of photos and images uploaded by users. There are lots of images you can use for free as the image owner must specify the license of each image. You need to carefully read the license of each image before using them and make sure they are allowed to be used for commercial or non-commercial use. I suggest you read this article on how to properly use and credit the images on Flickr http://www.squidoo.com/cc-flickr - Using Creative Common Images from Flickr. http://www.flickr.com/

Art.com - Thousands upon thousands of great art and poster prints that you can use on your websites. Simply link the images via your Art.com affiliate link to their website. http://www.art.com/

Pixabay.com - At Pixabay you will find thousands of high quality photos and images that are completely royalty free. You can use these images in any way you like. They don't require any credit attribution but as I always say - give credit where it's due. http://pixabay.com/

MorgueFile.com - Search MorgueFile for completely free quality images. These images can be used for both commercial and non-commercial purposes. You do not need to attribute the image author if you are not claiming ownership of the image or reselling them in its original state. http://www.morguefile.com/

Kozzi.com - FREE Kozzi Stock Images features over 75,000 completely free stock images and clipart for both commercial and personal use. You will need to register at Kozzi to download free images. http://www.kozzi.com/

Zazzle.com - Browse though millions of images on varied products to add to your websites. You will need to sign up as an Associate and use their link tools to properly and legally add Zazzle images on your websites that points back to their websites with your referral code. http://www.zazzle.com/

OpenPhoto.net - Royalty free stock photo site that you can download and even upload your own photos. You will need to register with the site to upload your own photos. http://www.openphoto.net/

RGBStock.com - Free fabulous stock photo download. You will need to register at RGBStock to gain access to their very good collection of quality images. You may the images you find here in digital format on websites, blogs, multimedia presentations, broadcast film and video or in printed material such as magazines, books, brochures, flyers and text books. http://www.rgbstock.com/

UnProfound.com - Lots of photos can be found here that you can use completely free. Photographers upload their work on this site and make it available for anyone to use for free. http://www.unprofound.com/

Public Domain Photos - The photos on this site is all in the public domain and you can use them for any purpose absolutely free. http://www.public-domain-photos.com/

Wikimedia Creative Commons - For the most part, most of the images here are in the public domain and you can use them royalty free. I suggest you give credit for any images you find here. Please read the terms and license for each image before using them in any way. http://commons.wikimedia.org/wiki/Main_Page

Historical Stock Photos - Great site to get free vintage stock photos and images. http://www.historicalstockphotos.com/

Stock.XCHNG - Lots of great free photos to download on several subjects. The site also features an easy search tool and lightbox where you can save your images for future access. http://www.sxc.hu/

FreePixels - Download free stock photos and images from FreePixels. They have a nice collection of business type images great for business related projects. http://www.freepixels.com/

FreeImages.co.uk - At FreeImages you'll find a library of stock photography for use on websites, printed media, products and anywhere you need a photo to help with illustration and design. 6,000+ stock photos that you can download. You need to credit the site for any images used. http://www.freeimages.co.uk/

ImageBase - Their royalty-free photos are licensed under creative commons and you can use the images here for both personal and business use. http://imagebase.davidniblack.com/main.php

Photo Rogue - Looking for something different? An image you can't find anywhere else? Why not make a request on this site and ask their professional photographers to go take that picture for you. http://www.photorogue.com/

Stock Vault - All images on this site are free for non-commercial use. They have a nice search function and also lightbox feature for registered users. http://www.stockvault.net/

Geek Philosopher - Lots of free photos, wallpaper and background images available here. You will need to give proper credit for the images used. http://geekphilosopher.com/MainPage/photos.htm

Pixel Perfect Digital - Good collection of stunning stock photos. You can use their images on your websites but not on any print media. They also have a good collection of cartoons and smiley faces. http://www.pixelperfectdigital.com/free_stock_photos/

Free Range Stock - You will need to register with this site to gain access to download tons of high quality stock images and textures. All images are at least 2400 x 1600, and photos can be used for commercial or personal projects. http://freerangestock.com/

Image After Free Images - ImageAfter is a large online free photo collection. You can download and use any image or texture from their site and use it in your own work, either personal or commercial work. http://www.imageafter.com/

FreeStock Photos - Lots of nice quality stock photos that you can use for free. Their photos have watermark on them that you must retain and give a link back to their site. http://freestockphotos.com/

FreeFoto - A big collection of stock photography that are available royalty-free. http://www.freefoto.com/index.jsp

PDPhoto - A very good site for public domain images. Credit and link need to be given for images used. http://www.pdphoto.org/

African wildlife Stock Photography - A good collection of animal, safari and African wildlife pictures. http://www.wildlife-pictures-online.com/free-stockpictures.html

BigFoto - Another big collection of quality images on many subjects. A link credit must be given for any images used. http://www.bigfoto.com/

Clker.com Royalty-Free Vector Clipart - Tons of very good graphics and clipart to use anywhere you want. http://www.clker.com/

51

FreeClipartFree - Huge collection of free clipart and graphics on many subjects. http://www.freeclipartfree.com/

U.S. Fish & Wildlife Service Digital Library - Big collection of images of birds, animals, fish and other wildlife. http://www.fws.gov/digitalmedia

National Oceanic and Atmospheric Administration - Lots of weather related photos and charts. - oceans, storms, forest fires and more. http://www.noaa.gov/

Discovery Education: Clip Art Gallery - Good free educational clipart and graphics for non-commercial and educational use. http://school.discoveryeducation.com/clipart/

NASA Image Library - Lots of space, planets and spacecraft images. http://www.nasa.gov/multimedia/imagegallery/

Nations Illustrated - Over 8,000 stock photos of places, monuments and much more. http://www.nationsillustrated.com/

U.S. National Park Photographs - Public domain photographs of America's national parks, animals, birds, fauna and flora. http://www.nps.gov/pub_aff/imagebase.html

White House Photo Gallery - U.S. Government related photos.
http://www.whitehouse.gov/photogallery

Cepolina - Royalty free stock images and photos. Over 20,000 photos in lots of categories. You can search for photos in several languages and pinpoint images you want from world maps.
http://www.cepolina.com/freephoto/

U.S. Government Photos and Images - A library sites of all U.S. Government and Agencies photos.
http://www.usa.gov/Topics/Graphics.shtml

Every Stock Photo - A good search engine site that will help you find royalty stock images from multiple sites. You can also search by different license types. http://www.everystockphoto.com/

Woophy - A wonderful collection of travel and places photographs. You can pinpoint any place on the map to look for images of that place. You can even rate photos and leave comments on them.
http://woophy.com/#&mag=1&lng=0.008441&lat=14.001683

Free Photo Bank - FreePhotoBank is a free stock photo site. Feel free to download pictures (up to 2048 pixels, Creative Commons license) but don't forget to link back to FreePhotoBank. Over 8,000 pictures on this site.
http://www.freephotobank.org/main.php

Karen Whimsy Public Domain Images - You will find hundreds of beautiful images gleaned from Karen's collection of old books, magazines, and postcards. They are all from material printed prior to 1923 and are in the public domain. Please read the simple and generous terms on the website before using any image. http://karenswhimsy.com/public-domain-images/

Image Envision - Royalty-Free Historical Graphics, Stock Photos, Illustrations, and Clipart Images. http://www.imageenvision.com/all-graphics/historical

Free Nature Pics - Lots of free nature pics, animals, flowers, mountains, lakes, forests, caves, skies and much more. All free but they require a link back to their site. http://www.freenaturepictures.com/

Kave Wall Stock - Free stock photos, images and textures. http://www.kavewall.com/stock/index.html

Free Travel Stock Photos - 3000+ free, travel-themed stock-images ready for instant download. Images are provided free of charge under a Creative Commons license - on a royalty free basis and the condition that a credit (printed use) or a hyperlink (online use) is made. http://photoeverywhere.co.uk/

Buy Stock Photos and Images

Sometimes the image you really want can't be found on other sites or are not available for you to use due to copyright and license terms. I recommend you also search the sites below to find exactly what you are looking for. They have a fantastic collection of high-quality stock photos, images, illustrations, vectors, textures, models and much more that you need to pay for to use the images legally for your projects. Each of these sites has different subscription fees, download limits and image costs and you need to check them out properly before signing up.

GettyImages.com - Leading provider of digital media worldwide, creating and distributing a range of assets - from royalty-free stock photography and editorial images to video, music and multimedia - that help communicators around the globe tell their stories. http://www.gettyimages.com/

iStockPhoto.com - Lots of high quality stock photos, illustrations, videos, audios and much more. http://www.istockphoto.com/

ShutterStock.com - Over 20 million stock photos, illustrations, vectors and videos. http://www.shutterstock.com/

DreamsTime.com - Download Royalty-Free stock photos, illustrations & images for as low as $0.20 / image or free. http://www.dreamstime.com/

Fotolia.com - Royalty Free Images, Vectors and Videos from $0.74. Add impact to your design projects with royalty-free images from Fotolia. All licenses include unlimited print runs and never expire! http://www.fotolia.com/

I Have a Special Gift for My Readers

I appreciate my readers for without them I am just another author attempting to make a difference.

My readers and I have in common a passion for the written word as well as the desire to learn and grow from books.

My special offer to you is a massive ebook library that I have compiled over the years. It contains hundreds of fiction and non-fiction ebooks in Adobe Acrobat PDF format as well as the Greek classics and old literary classics too.

In fact, this library is so massive to completely download the entire library will require over 5 GBs open on your desktop.

Use the link below and scan all of the ebooks in the library. You can select the ebooks you want individually or download the entire library.

The link below does not expire after a given time period so you are free to return for more books rather than clog your desktop. And feel free to give the link to your friends who enjoy reading too.

I thank you for reading my book and hope if you are pleased that you will leave me an honest review so that I can improve my work and or write books that appeal to your interests.

Okay, here is the link…

http://tinyurl.com/special-readers-promo

PS: If you wish to reach me personally for any reason you may simply write to mailto:support@epubwealth.com.

I answer all of my emails so rest assured I will respond.

Meet the Author

Dr. Leland Benton is Director of Applied Web Info, a holding company for ePubWealth.com, a leading ePublisher company based in Utah. With over 21,000 resellers in over 22-countries, ePubWealth.com is a leader in ePublishing, book promotion, and ebook marketing.

As the creator and author of "The ePubWealth Program," Leland teaches up-and-coming authors the ins-and-outs of today's ePublishing world. He has assisted hundreds of authors make it big in the ePublishing world.

Leland also created a series of external book promotion programs and teaches authors how to promote their books using external marketing sources.

Leland is also the Managing Director of Applied Mind Sciences, the company's mind research unit and Chief Forensics Investigator for the company's ForensicsNation unit. He is active in privacy rights through the company's PrivacyNations unit and is an expert in survival planning and disaster relief through the company's SurvivalNations unit.

Leland resides in Southern Utah.

Visit some of his websites
http://www.AddMeInNow.com
http://www.AppliedMindSciences.com
http://www.BookbuilderPLUS.com
http://www.BookJumping.com
http://www.EmailNations.com
http://www.EmbarrassingProblemsFix.com
http://www.ePubWealth.com
http://www.ForensicsNation.com
http://www.ForensicsNationStore.com
http://www.FreebiesNation.com
http://www.HealthFitnessWellnessNation.com
http://www.Neternatives.com
http://www.PrivacyNations.com
http://www.RetireWithoutMoney.org
http://www.SurvivalNations.com
http://www.TheBentonKitchen.com
http://www.Theolegions.org
http://www.VideoBookbuilder.com